PIANO • VOCAL • GUITAR

TOP ▶ REQUESTS
Irish MUSIC

21 POPULAR AND TRADITIONAL FAVORITES

Contents

Produced by
Alfred Music Publishing Co., Inc.
P.O. Box 10003
Van Nuys, CA 91410-0003
alfred.com

Printed in USA.

ISBN-10: 0-7390-9421-1
ISBN-13: 978-0-7390-9421-1

Cover photo: Kilcoe Castle, Ireland © Shutterstock / Patrick Kosmider

Alfred Cares. Contents printed on 100% recycled paper.

THE BLACK VELVET BAND

Traditional Irish Folk Song

Moderately (♩. = 60)   *Verse:*

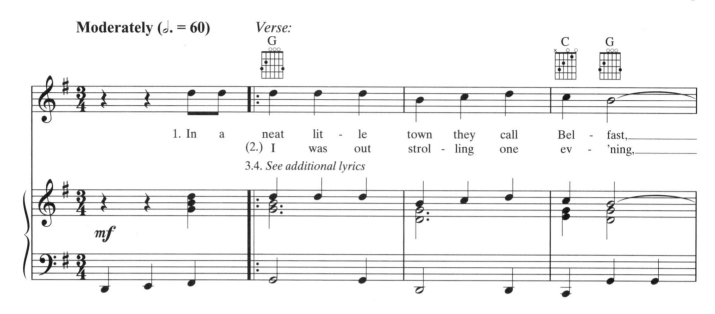

1. In a neat lit - tle town they call Bel - fast,_____
(2.) I was out strol - ling one ev - 'ning,_____
3.4. *See additional lyrics*

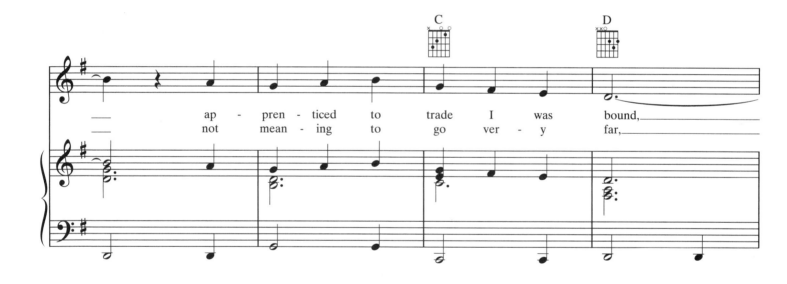

ap - pren - ticed to trade I was bound,_____
not mean - ing to go ver - y far,_____

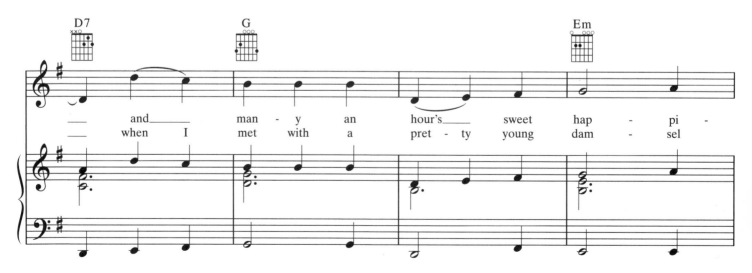

and_____ man - y an hour's_____ sweet hap - pi -
when I met with a pret - ty young dam - sel

Chorus:

tions, to fol - low the black vel - vet band._____

son; bad luck to the black ve - vet band._____

Her eyes, they shone like the dia - monds,_____

_____ you'd think she was queen of the land._____

_____ And her hair hung o - ver her shoul -

der,   tied   up   with   a   black   vel - vet   band.

2. Well,
3. Next
4. So

band.

Verse 3:
Next morning, before judge and jury
For a trial I had to appear.
And the judge, he said, "You young fellows...
The case against you is quite clear.
And seven long years is your sentence,
You're going to Van Dieman's Land,
Far away from your friends and relations
To follow the black velvet band."
(To Chorus:)

Verse 4:
So come, all you jolly young fellows,
I'd have you take warning by me,
Whenever you're out on the liquor, me lads,
Beware of the pretty colleen.
She'll fill you with whiskey and porter
Until you're unable to stand,
And the very next thing that you'll know, me lads,
You're landed in Van Dieman's Land.
(To Chorus:)

CLANCY LOWERED THE BOOM

Words and Music by
JOHNNY LANGE and
HY HEATH

Brightly (♩. = 120)

1. Now

Verse:

Clan - cy was a peace - ful man, if you know what I mean._____ The
(2.) O'Lear - y was a fight - ing man; they all knew he was tough._____ He
(3.) Clan - cy left the bar - ber - shop with ton - ic on his hair._____ He

4.5.6. *See additional lyrics*

cops picked up the piec - es af - ter Clan - cy left the scene._____ He
strut - ted 'round the neigh - bor - hood a - shoot - in' off his guff._____ He
walked in - to the pool room, and he met O - 'Ri - ley there._____ O -

Verse 4:
Mulrooney walked into the bar and ordered up a round.
He left his drink to telephone, and Clancy drank it down.
Mulrooney said, "Who drunk me drink? I'll lay him in the tomb!"
Before you could pat the top of your hat,
Clancy lowered the boom!
(To Chorus:)

Verse 5:
O'Hollihan delivered ice to Misses Clancy's flat.
He'd always linger for a while to talk of this and that.
One day he kissed her just as Clancy walked into the room.
Before you could say the time of day,
Clancy lowered the boom!
(To Chorus:)

Verse 6:
The neighbors all turned out for Kate O'Grady's wedding night.
McDugal said, "Let's have some fun, I think I'll start a fight!"
He wrecked the hall, then kissed the bride, and pulverized the groom.
Then quick as a wink, before you could think,
Clancy lowered the boom!
(To Chorus:)

I'LL TAKE YOU HOME AGAIN, KATHLEEN

Words and Music by
THOMAS P. WESTENDORF

Andante, con espressione (♩ = 80-84)

1. I'll   take   you home a-gain, Kath - leen,_____ a - cross the o - cean wild and
(2.) know   you love me, Kath-leen, dear,_____ your heart was ev - er fond and
(3.) that   dear home be-yond the sea_____ my Kath - leen shall a - gain re-

wide,_____ to where your heart had al - ways been,_____ since
true._____ I al - ways feel, when you are near,_____ that
turn._____ And when .thy old friends wel - come thee,_____ thy

10

COCKLES AND MUSSELS (MOLLY MALONE)

Traditional Irish Song

DANNY BOY
(Londonderry Air)

Traditional

Andante

THE IRISH ROVER

Traditional Irish Folk Song

1. In the year of our Lord, eight - een hun - dred and six, we set sail from the coal quay of
(2.) one mil - lion bags of the best Sli - go rags. We had two mil - lion bar - rels of
(3.) Mick - ey Coote who played hard on his flute. And the la - dies lined up for a
4.5. *See additional lyrics*

Cork. We were sail - ing a - way with a car - go of bricks for the grand Cit - y Hall in New
bones. We had three mil - lion sides of old blind hors - es' hides. We had four mil - lion bar - rels of
set. He would too - tle with skill for each spark - ling quad - rille, though the danc - ers were fluth - ered and

York. We'd an el - e - gant craft, it was rigged fore and aft, and how the trade winds
stones. We had five mil - lion hogs and six mil - lion dogs, sev - en mil - lion bar - rels of
bet. With his smart wit - ty talk, he was cock of the walk as he rolled the dames un - der and

drove_____ her. She had twen - ty-three masts, and she stood sev - 'ral blasts, and they
por - ter. We had eight mil - lion bales of old nan - ny goats' tails in the
o - ver. They all knew at a glance, when he took up his stance, that he

called her the I - rish Ro - ver. 2. We had Ro - ver.
hold of the I - rish Ro - ver. 3. There was
sailed in the I - rish Ro - ver. 4. There was

Verse 4:
There was Barney McGee from the banks of the Lee.
There was Hogan from County Tyrone.
There was Johnny McGurk who was scared stiff of work,
And a man from Westmeath called Malone.
There was Slugger O'Toole who was drunk as a rule,
And fighting Bill Tracy from Dover.
And your man, Mick McCann, from the banks of the Bann
Was the skipper of the Irish Rover.

Verse 5:
We had sailed seven years when the measles broke out,
And the ship lost its way in the fog.
And that whale of a crew was reduced down to two:
Just myself and the Captain's old dog.
Then the ship struck a rock. Oh Lord! What a shock!
The bulkhead was turned right over,
Turned nine times around and the poor dog was drowned.
I'm the last of the Irish Rover.

THE IRISH WASHERWOMAN

Traditional Irish Jig

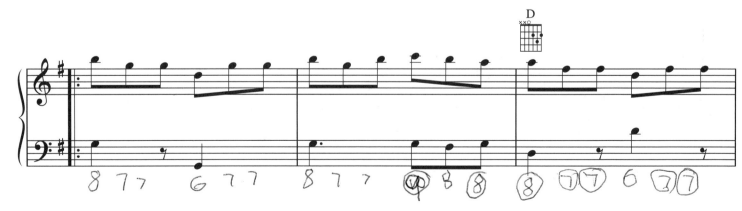

The Irish Washerwoman - 2 - 1

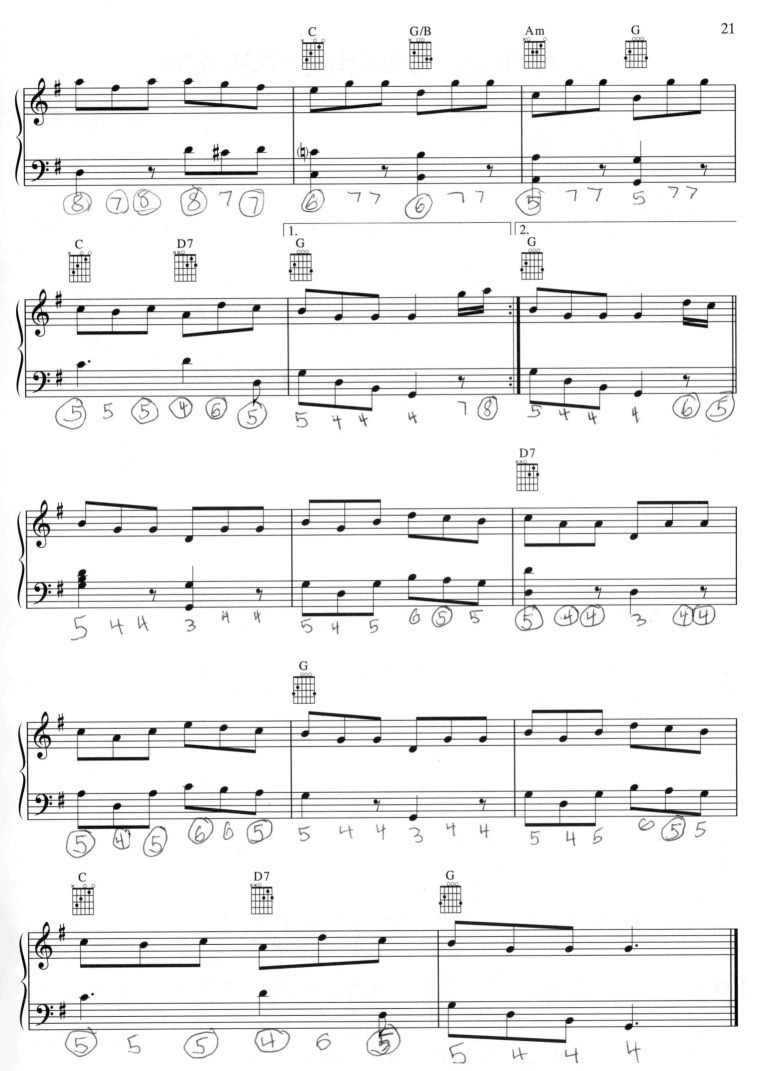

IT'S A GREAT DAY FOR THE IRISH

Words and Music by
ROGER EDENS

Moderately, March tempo

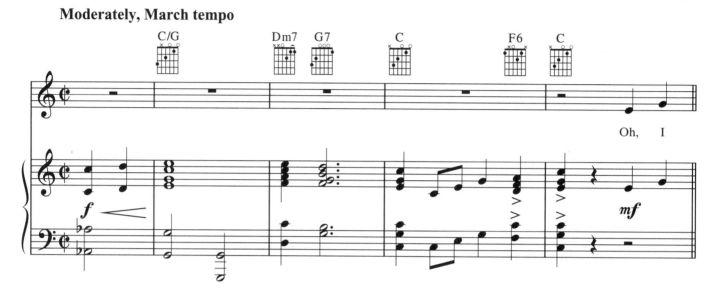

Oh, I

Verse:

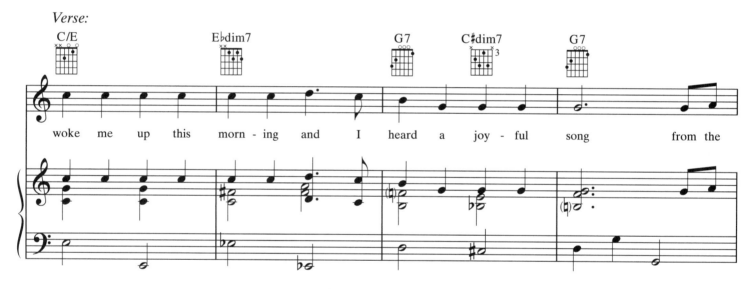

woke me up this morn - ing and I heard a joy - ful song from the

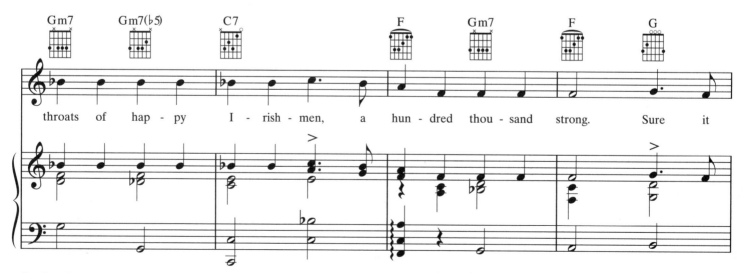

throats of hap - py I - rish - men, a hun - dred thou - sand strong. Sure it

It's a Great Day for the Irish - 4 - 1

It's a Great Day for the Irish - 4 - 4

THE IRISH WEDDING SONG

(The Wedding Song)

Words and Music by
IAN BETTERIDGE

Moderate, gentle waltz

Verse:

1. (T)Here they
2. May they
3. As they

stand, hand in hand, they've ex - changed wed - ding bands. To the
find peace of mind know comes to all love who are kind. May the
go, may they know ev - 'ry that was shown. And as

day is the day____ of all their dreams and their plans.____ And
rough times a - head____ be - come____ short - er, may their tri - umphs in feel - ings time.____ Wher -
life it gets short - er, may their feel - ings grow.____

The Irish Wedding Song - 3 - 1

all of their loved ones are here to say;_____ Oh,
May_____ their chil - dren be hap - py each day._____
ev - er they trav - el, wher - ev - er they stay,_____ may

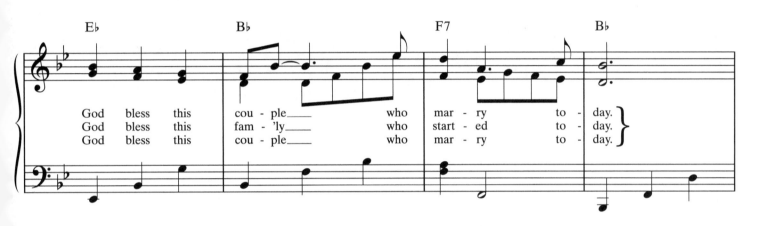

God bless this cou - ple_____ who mar - ry to - day.
God bless this fam - 'ly_____ who start - ed to - day.
God bless this cou - ple_____ who mar - ry to - day.

Chorus:

In good times and bad times, in sick - ness and

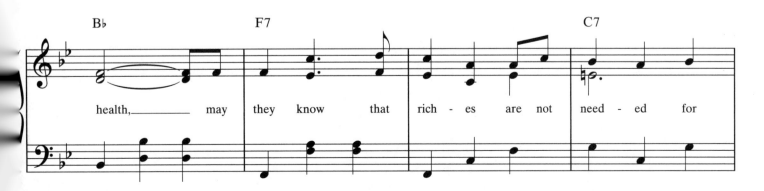

health,_____ may they know that rich - es are not need - ed for

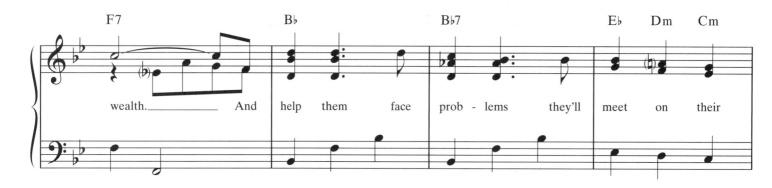

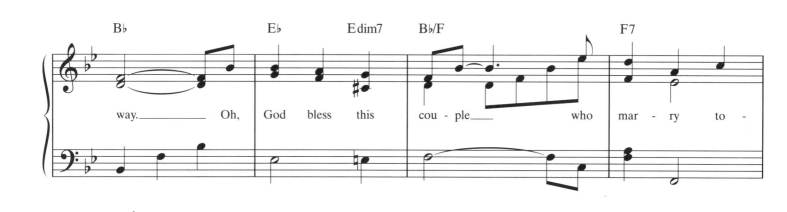

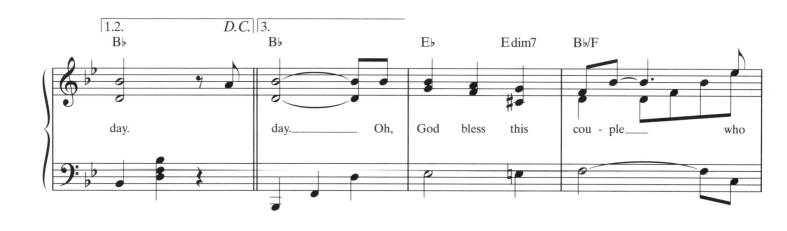

Much slower

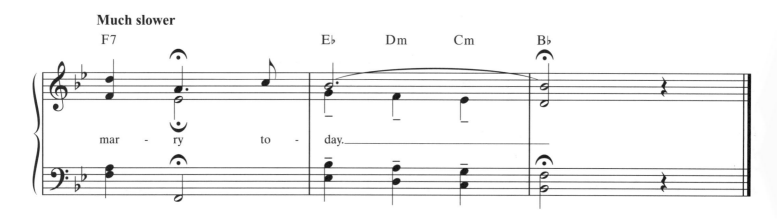

MOTHER MACHREE

Words and Music by
CHANCELLOR OLCOTT

1. There's a spot in my heart which no col - leen may own, there's a
2. Ev - 'ry sor - row or care in the dear days gone by was made

depth in my soul nev - er sound - ed or known. There's a
bright by the light of the smile in your eye. Like a

Mother Machree - 3 - 1

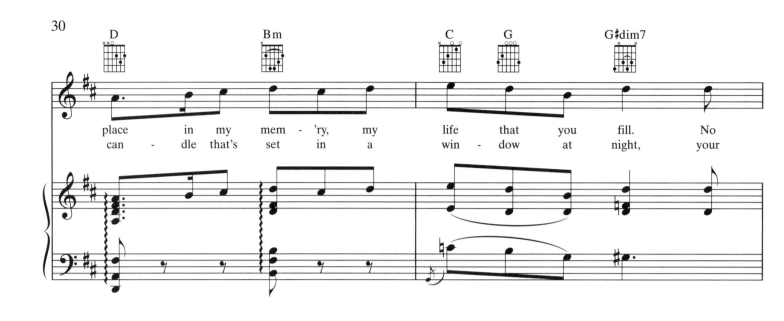

place in my mem - 'ry, my life that you fill. No
can - dle that's set in a win - dow at night, No your

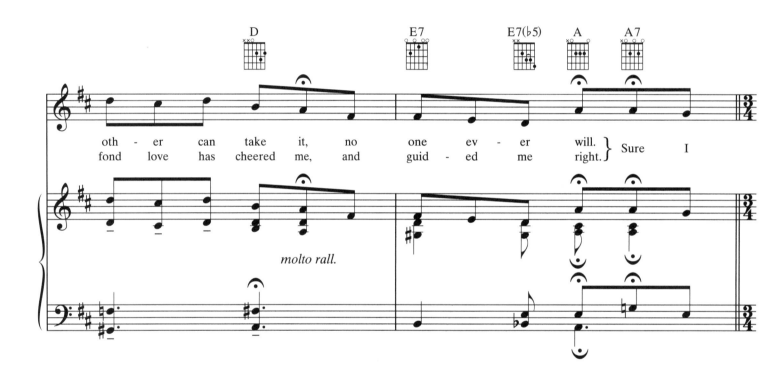

oth - er can take it, no one ev - er will. } Sure I
fond love has cheered me, and guid - ed me right. }

molto rall.

Tenderly, with much expression

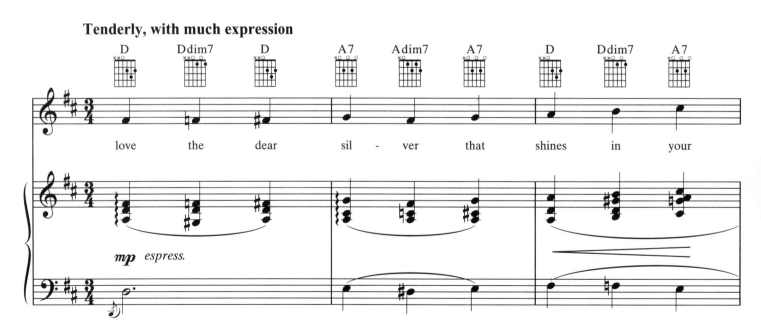

love the dear sil - ver that shines in your

mp espress.

THE KERRY DANCE

Traditional Irish Song

Verses 1, 2, & 4:

1. O the days of the Ker - ry danc - ing, o the ring of the pi - per's tune!
2. Was there ev - er a sweet - er col - leen in the dance___ than Ei - ly Moore!
4. Lov - ing voi - ces of old com - pan - ions, steal - ing out of the past once more.

O for one of those hours of glad - ness, gone, a - las, like our youth, too soon:
Or a proud - er lad than Tha - dy, as he bold - ly took the floor:
And the sound of the dear old mu - sic, soft and sweet as in days of yor:

The Kerry Dance - 4 - 1

THE LAST ROSE OF SUMMER

Lyrics by
THOMAS MOORE

Traditional Irish Melody

MY WILD IRISH ROSE

Words and Music by
CHANCELLOR "CHAUNCEY" OLCOTT

My Wild Irish Rose - 4 - 4

THE PARTING GLASS

Traditional Irish Folk Song

Freely (♩ = 112)

1. Of___ all the mon - ey that e'er I had, I've___ spent it in___ good___
(2.) I had mon - ey e - nough to spend, and___ lei - sure time to
(3.) all the com - rades that e'er I had, they're___ sor - ry for___ my

com - pa - ny. And___ all the harm that___ ever I did, a -
sit a while, there___ is a fair maid___ in the town who___
going a - way. And___ all the sweet - hearts that e'er I had, they'd___

las, 'twas done___ to___ none but me. And all___ I've___ done for
sore - ly has___ my___ heart be - guiled. Her ros - y___ cheeks and
wish me one___ more___ day to stay. But since___ it___ falls un -

a tempo

43

The Parting Glass - 2 - 2

THE ROCKY ROAD TO DUBLIN

Traditional Irish Folk Song

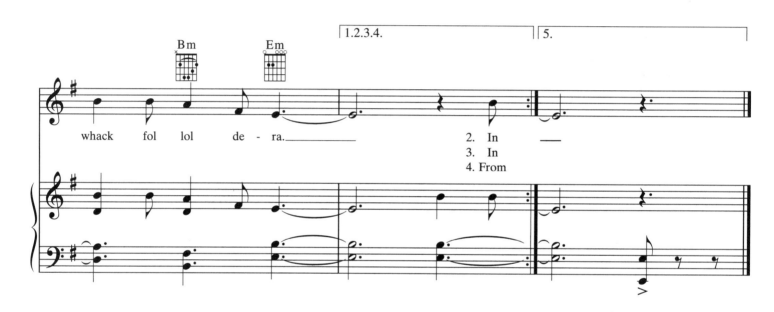

Verse 4:
From there I got away, me spirits never failing.
Landed on the quay, just as the ship was sailing.
The Captain at me roared; said no room had he.
When I jumped aboard, a cabin found for Paddy
Down among the pigs; played some funny rigs.
Danced some hearty jigs, the water 'round me bubbling.
When off to Holhead, wished meself was dead,
Or better far instead on the rocky road to Dublin.
(To Chorus:)

Verse 5:
The boys of Liverpool, when we were safely landed
Called meself a fool. I could no longer stand it.
Blood began to boil, temper I was losing.
Poor old Erin's Isle, they began abusing.
"Hurrah me soul!" says I. Let the shillelagh fly.
Some Galway boys were nigh and saw I was a hobblin'.
With a loud "Hurray!" joined in the fray.
Soon we cleared the way on the rocky road to Dublin.
(To Chorus:)

SEVEN DRUNKEN NIGHTS

Traditional Irish Folk Song

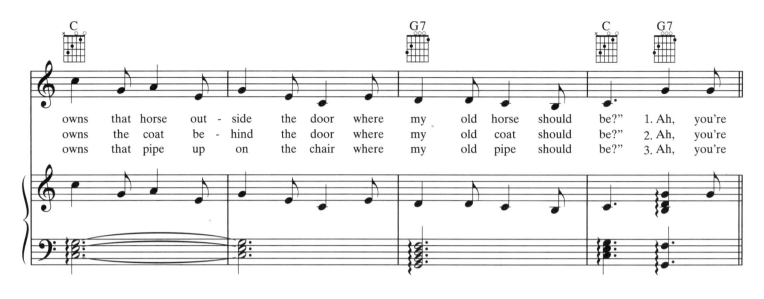

owns that horse out-side the door where my old horse should be?" 1. Ah, you're
owns the coat be-hind the door where my old coat should be?" 2. Ah, you're
owns that pipe up on the chair where my old pipe should be?" 3. Ah, you're

Chorus:

drunk, you're drunk, you sil-ly old fool, so drunk you can-not see._____ And
drunk, you're drunk, you sil-ly old fool, so drunk you can-not see._____
drunk, you're drunk, you sil-ly old fool, so drunk you can-not see._____

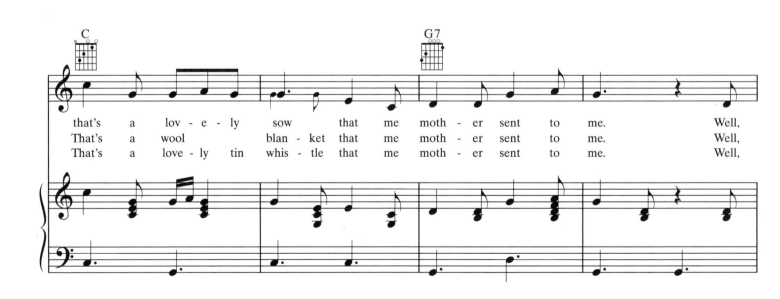

that's a lov-e-ly sow that me moth-er sent to me. Well,
That's a wool blan-ket that me moth-er sent to me. Well,
That's a love-ly tin whis-tle that me moth-er sent to me. Well,

Verse 4:
And as I went home on Thursday night as drunk as drunk could be,
I saw two boots beneath the bed where my old boots should be.
Well, I called me wife and I said to her, "Will ya kindly tell to me
Who owns them boots beneath the bed where my old boots should be?"
(To Chorus 4):

Chorus 4:
Ah, you're drunk, you're drunk, you silly old fool,
So drunk you cannot see.
They're two lovely geranium pots me mother sent to me.
Well, it's many a day I've travelled a hundred miles or more.
But laces in geranium pots I never saw before.

Verse 5:
And as I went home on Friday night as drunk as drunk could be,
I saw a head upon the bed where my old head should be.
Well, I called me wife and I said to her, "Will ya kindly tell to me
Who owns that head upon the bed where my old head should be?"
(To Chorus 5):

Chorus 5:
Ah, you're drunk, you're drunk, you silly old fool,
So drunk you cannot see.
That's a baby boy that me mother sent to me.
Well, it's many a day I've travelled a hundred miles or more.
But a baby boy with his whiskers on sure I never saw before.

Verse 6:
And as I went home on Saturday night as drunk as drunk could be,
I saw two hands upon her breasts where my old hands should be.
Well, I called me wife and I said to her, "Will ya kindly tell to me
Who owns them hands upon your breasts where my old hands should be?"
(To Chorus 6):

Chorus 6:
Ah, you're drunk, you're drunk, you silly old fool,
So drunk you cannot see.
That's a lovely night gown that me mother sent to me.
Well, it's many a day I've travelled a hundred miles or more.
But fingers in a night gown sure I never saw before.

Verse 7:
And as I went home on Sunday night as drunk as drunk could be,
I saw a lad sneaking out the back a quarter after three.
Well, I called me wife and I said to her, "Will ya kindly tell to me
Who was that lad sneaking out the back a quarter after three?"
(To Chorus 7):

Chorus 7:
Ah, you're drunk, you're drunk, you silly old fool,
So drunk you cannot see.
That was just the tax man that the Queen, she sent to me.
Well, it's many a day I've travelled a hundred miles or more.
But an Englishman who can last till three I've never seen before.

THE WEARING OF THE GREEN

Traditional Irish Ballad

Moderately, with expression

Lyrics:

1. Oh, Paddy, dear, and did you hear the news that's go-in' 'round? The Sham-rock is for-bid by law to grow on I-rish ground. Saint

since the col-or we must wear is Eng-land's cru-el red, sure Ire-land's sons will ne'er for-get the blood that they have shed. You may

if at last our col-or should be torn from Ire-land's heart, her sons with shame and sor-row from the dear old sod will part. I've heard

52

The Wearing of the Green - 3 - 3

THE WILD ROVER

Roud Folk Song

Chorus:

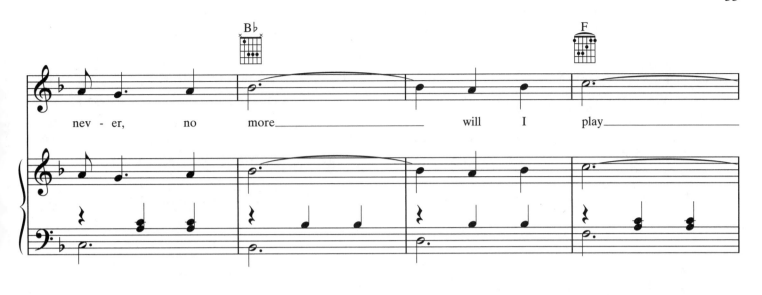

never, no more_____ will I play_____

____ the wild ro-ver,_____ no, nev-er,_____

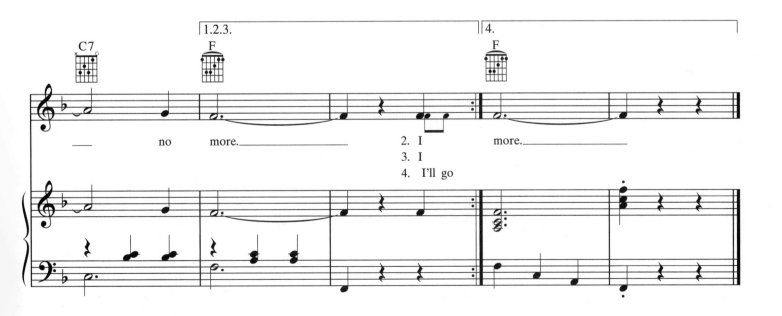

____ no more._____ 2. I more._____
3. I
4. I'll go

WHEN IRISH EYES ARE SMILING

Words by
CHAUNCEY OLCOTT
and GEORGE GRAFF, JR.

Music by
ERNEST R. BALL

57

When Irish Eyes Are Smiling - 2 - 2

WHISKEY IN THE JAR

Traditional Irish Folk Song

Verse 4:
'Twas early in the morning, as I rose up for the travel.
The guards were all around me, and likewise Captain Farrel.
I first produced my pistol, for she stole my rapier.
But I couldn't shoot the water, so a prisoner I was taken.
(To Chorus:)

Verse 5:
If anyone can aid me, it's my brother in the army.
If I can find his station down in Cork or in Killarney.
And if he'll come and save me, we'll go roving in Kilkenny.
I swear he'll treat me better than my darling sportling, Jenny.
(To Chorus:)

Verse 6:
Now, some men take delight in the drinking and the roving.
But others take delight in the gambling and the smoking.
Now, I take delight in the juice of the barley.
And courting pretty fair maids in the morning bright and early.
(To Chorus:)

YOU RAISE ME UP

Words and Music by
ROLF LOVLAND and
BRENDAN GRAHAM

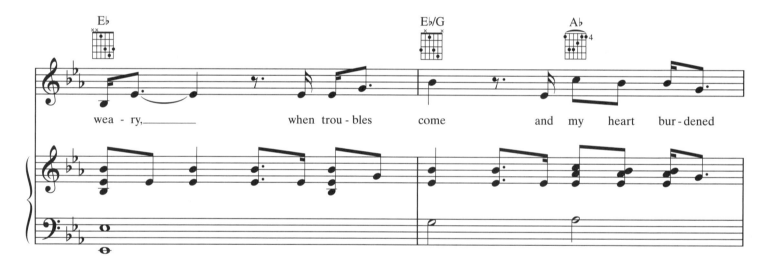

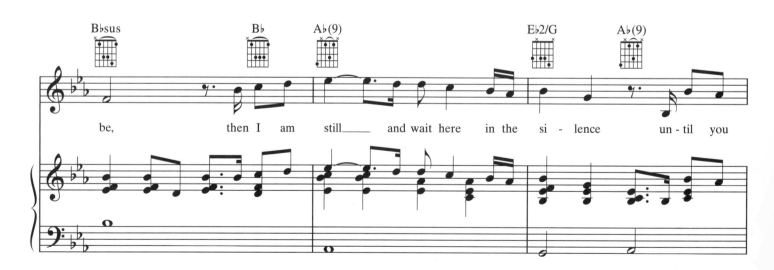

You Raise Me Up - 5 - 1

64

You Raise Me Up - 5 - 5